between you
and these bones

between you
and these bones

F. D. Soul

Andrews McMeel
PUBLISHING®

Andrews McMeel Publishing
a division of Andrews McMeel Universal
1130 Walnut Street, Kansas City, Missouri 64106

www.andrewsmcmeel.com

19 20 21 22 23 BVG 10 9 8 7 6 5 4 3 2 1
ISBN: 978-1-5248-5060-9
Library of Congress Control Number: 2019931739

Illustrations by Elliana Esquivel

Editor: Patty Rice
Designer/Art Director: Spencer Williams
Production Editor: Amy Strassner
Production Manager: Carol Coe

between you and
these bones

For Libby

I am naked to the waist and there is a forest fire starting beneath my ear. you are up against the mirror. kindling.

If you are thinking this is not what an intelligent person would put into a book that will be read by her grandmother. by her boyfriend's parents. (let alone start with it.) then you are right.

The thing about being called a poet is that you can do fiendishly outrageous things and call it art. a little-known fact is that authors eat dictionaries for breakfast and still do not put on weight. also, bumblebees sleep underground. google it.

On Sunday I etched words onto the back of my ankle. nearly gave my father an aneurysm with this small act of defiance. my great "ha!" to a future in which me as I am now no longer owns this body.

What I mean to say is that my high school English teacher told me *you must write with structure until you become an author, at which point you may do as you please.* which is to say that I can start without a capital and no one will fist fight me.

For some reason I do not believe in washing pajamas. or
getting a new toothbrush at a hygienically appropriate time.

which is to say that what I do believe is that all living is
some form of rebellion. some form of art.

some form of printing poetry out across your skin in the
hopes of waking up under a wood and brass doorframe
where the nameplate reads

                    home.

                                        j. d. soul

CONTENTS

I

POETRY FOR THE NONBELIEVER

Here.
I do not want you to read this
hard and heavy-handed.
The problem is you keep trying to use your eyes, my
love. See.
How I use the word
gently
as if this is only a poem and not all of me wrapped
tightly around all of you.

The First Explanation:
this is
rain on the roof
the freckles across your collarbone
braille.
When you touch the skin by my waist and call me
soft, this is what I hear.

Remember when I stood in the fountain
and looked up
traced constellations that were only city lights
marveled at the weary in my hands.

Remember how I wouldn't come out
and the night was cold
and tired
and maybe I was trying to show you
how the hours can drag on and on
if you let them
and
on and on if you don't.

The Second:
I am teaching you piano
and when I hold your fingers to my mouth
whisper
slower this time
what I mean is
good poetry is closing your eyes when you hear my
heartbeat and wonder if it is your own.
Finding it in the pauses. In the hollow of my neck.
How I soften when you pull me against you.
And in exchange
you are teaching me to love
(although you do not know this yet).

I want you to read this under that waterfall with my
lips turning the color of the water
and your heart
threatening mutiny.

I will pretend that I have not already heard the
question in your eyes. That
you do not already feel like home to me.
And so you ask,
because you are a gentleman
and afraid

and your voice is poetry
and your mouth is poetry
and the way your eyes can hold
so much light
and me all at once.

The Third:
it is you.

It is a wonderful, terrifying thing.
to take out your throat and
hand it to a stranger.

CARMEN CYGNI

You perhaps will become my swan song
I think
I feel the spines of my grandmother's books in you
the heavy kind
the padding lightly across a silent hallway
a tiptoe
because the books are *adult*
and I am only small
and because the floorboards are shy,
but awfully loud.

In your house there is a radio
that never sleeps
welcomes me in to
stamp off my boots and clutter up
the quiet
on gentle, dewy mornings
crane your neck and you can hear
the lawn gurgling and laughing away
and in summer you will dip your toes in
cool the backs of your knees on her
and oh,
how much space there is to breathe
and feel beautiful here.

what I am trying to say is that
when I was younger I prayed
quiet as a breath
for a boy
who looked like kindness and
felt like home

and my God,

how you are him.

BECOME

It is a very human thing
to love
and let that become our poetry

so long as the love is always first
for us.

The day will break open.
roaring and wild as if it had never left.
and you,
love,
oh, I hope you do the same.

FIVE LOAVES AND TWO FISH

For me, home is my grandmother's hands. 6 a.m.
nestled into the smell of bread, and the braid like
spun silk that spills down the back of her nightgown.

My grandfather escaped the war. became a sheep
farmer instead. stamped off the smell of cold boots
and lanolin at the door each day, precisely at noon.
brought us the orphans if we were lucky. scoffed
when we named them. sniffy. snowy. daisy. sweet,
bleating little things with muddy wagging tails.

My grandmother is the only person I've ever known
to cook each day ready to feed a small army. five
loaves and two fish. The whole house constantly
smelling like Christmas. like hands wiped on an
apron and then caught up in your hair and around
your back. the weight of generations.

It's a new house now. with new wallpaper and new
floors and no secret penciled heights on the back of
the office door. My grandfather has an internet router
to cuss at, and my grandmother three new rooms to
fill up with the smell of her. a new stretch of bench
already etched and painted on by small sets of hands.

I still visit during break. when I need to feel small
and safe in the overdressed bed at the end of the hall.
learn sewing or the art of staying in love.

Slower limbs live there now. later mornings with no
yawning farm to attend to. more yelling about lost
remotes and lost hearing aids. but still, the hands that
rub home back into shoulder blades. tuck it under the
corners of my duvet. whisper it before turning out
the light like I am school-aged, and there is nothing in
the world more important to carry with me than this.

I

There are few things as sweet as a soft June sky
the way the rain always comes late
like an apology
hovers in the air awhile
kisses the tips of your ears.

You.
You are my good days.

THE FILLING

When I was young and afraid of the dark, my mother
taught me business. the fine art of the ponytail and
being extraordinary.

which is to say I have been loved dearly.

I still
have an affinity for balloons and tight spaces duvets
like great mountains the soft light of the hallway at my
grandparents'.

still look both ways cross toes for luck practice winking
when no one is looking.

At some point I left fear up in the attic with the bag of
half-used fabric and old Christmas cards, forgot to go
back for it.

pierced my ears. learned forgiveness and time
management skills. discovered taxes. discovered the
kind of love that curls up on the pillow next to you.
knows the word *whole*. stays until morning. makes
pancakes.

Line up the letters in height order.
tip them like laundry from your limbs
and call this living.
pour out poetry with the newborn's bathwater, with
the yawning daybreak and call this
home.

A VOW

I promise
you will not always be this war.

HOW WE START

You tell me there are too many kids dying these days.
that you have had depression for years.
you offer this
in the same way that you hold out your bag of hot chips
tell me I am all bones and
ask what I am doing at the beach in the middle of a
Thursday.

I am studying medicine and
a kid
and so, you ask me like it belongs to me.
you are eighty-seven
and your soft old eyes have held a war
the downfall of an economy
and four children who are now older than I am.

you ask me why they are dying and
how do we fix it
and James, sweet soul
I do not know.
but I think that perhaps
you
your easy chatter about the sun, how shiny the new
fish and chip shop's paint is,

how your antidepressants bring out the spring colors so
nicely
how your wife would have just loved this if she were still
alive
I think
that perhaps this is how we start.

A NOTE FROM BOOK ONE

Thank God for the stubbornness
of organs.

FOOTNOTES

It is four in the morning and you have just placed three pebbles up my spine. three small round pebbles like question marks.

which is to say secrets. whispers so quiet your lips brush my skin.

three small round promises.

It takes me seven days to stop being in love with you.

three small wishes.

On the way home we sing as many old songs as we can remember.

three footnotes.

We do not sing well, but we do sing hard, which is very nearly the same thing.

My boyfriend does not
speak in poems.
just
wakes up with them
all caught up in his hair.

MORVEN

I think I need to wear a dress for a while. fish
from a river near my father
talk more
to old friends like I know them
still
grass-stain my knees kiss you
swim until my lips blue
hold my breath
sit at the back of the church.

The wood of the pew will be hard
like starched linen
like growing pains
but you can see the window from there
and it will feel like home.
let the hymns stir up like dust motes
from your bones.

whisper
and tell yourself it isn't
prayer.

Glory eyes, there will always be another day.
there will always be another mercy.

HELLO AGAIN

Hello again,
dear one. comfort.
I write this like it is not an apology.
try to.
I have been away traveling. away at work. out.
poetry is my fifth limb, but a tiring one.
a dragging ankle.
still she comes back and I have been holding my breath.
she is tiring but
today I slept in until a quarter past eleven and
even then did not leave the blankets.
called in sick to work and meant
my belly is getting full again and the poetry
will not wait forever.

YOUR MOUTH IS A WARM THING

Your mouth is a warm thing
a prayer at the wrist inside of elbow shoulder collar
plum pit of neck
you are tongue
promise
tying knots in cherry stems
throat back of ear jaw missed mouth temple
whisper
you
sternum breast ribs waist
are every home
belly scar soft down of hair
I have ever looked for
curve of thigh knee calf ankle
and never found.

SOCK-MUTED FOOTFALL

I like to think I'm someone else's
half-awake
dreams softly piled up in their hair
still

you used to tell me warm hands
meant a good night's
sleep
how the day will creep up
all sock-muted footfall
how she makes you throw open the shutters
let the rain in
hold your mouth open for it.

I hope you forever leave the sheets untucked
just in case
or at least so that the night tumbles out
giddy and soft
onto the floorboards.

ON OTHER TONGUES

These poems are stolen things
a whisper on the bus
and I will bring it home to you
press it into a coat pocket.
There is an old man humming a tune and I am learning
it by heart so that tonight I can tell you
of his language and how
I cannot speak it but will never stop trying.

THE LAND THAT WRAPS AROUND YOU

Sarah / open cracked dry earth hot wet as a mouth as
the West as ink / stained cuffs freckled knees folded
edges tucked in collars bottoms of pockets / bookstore
promise / kerchief in ironclad helmet sweat breastplate
/ shells that are kept by the hundreds and never used for
anything / filling of drawers / you are more inhale ocean
bowhead whale / feeling through 3 a.m. with your
hands / finding the milk in the fridge the hallway light
on the warm side of the bed / the land that wraps
around you like an echo / elbows toothpicks leaving
hairpins everywhere inconvenient / rising with the
steady swell of the day pouring in through the windows
/ Hemlock blue spruce baby's breath / desert / I hope
you never find the place without enough poetry for the
two of you / Rosangela.

Perhaps I will take up dancing again.
loving with both hands.
biting lips harder
and singing while we make breakfast.

eggs and pancakes and
your mouth on my neck.

PRETTY LITTLE DISASTER YOU

What a pretty little disaster you will be
my love
God, I am terrified for you
I just know that I'll take your pressed petal
hands to my mouth
and cry for your skin
and cry for the hormones
and probably won't stop crying for years
and you

I hope you love like my mother
skip stones
always run farther than you are able
paint badly, and bake
laugh and get it all over everything
find a pair of soft hands
to pick yourself back up into
(I hope they are your father's for both our sakes)
be endlessly kind

sweet frightening one
I hope you love it here. I think that perhaps
I am only just learning to. but truly,
I do.

POETRY IN THE PASSENGER SEAT

I found poetry in the passenger seat yesterday.
in the roads stretched out in longing.
an arched back of asphalt.
in the day,
incessantly breaking herself
open for me.

A LOVE LETTER TO TODAY

Today I am thankful because my skin is kind and clean
and sometimes holds yours.

This morning carried autumn with her like a prayer
like a gentling
and tomorrow the rain will come
and I will follow.

I am thankful because the days will hold me tight
and if you stand still next to the lawn
you can hear her inhale
and you have lungs too, if you listen hard enough.

I am thankful because tonight the sky is kindling
and the words and you
are burning at my fingertips.

The trees by the porch have started their yawning and I
will keep pieces of them in the hot water cupboard.
I will bring them out like freshly folded sheets
carmine and vermilion
in memory of this whispering sky.

I will lose feeling in my hands
when the cold comes.
I will fold inside of myself.
June was never one of the good ones
but still

today
I am thankful.

The bravery it takes
to have you up against my skin like this.

I LEFT YOU AND MY BEST HEELS ON THE CONCRETE

There's a new sculpture down by the viaduct. they've
made it to look like a building.
like the word
                    architecture

but it doesn't. too polite. too easy to swing off of.
too much like that pond from when we
were kids and laughing.

I left you and my best heels on the concrete
waded in
they can't get me here
they can't
and I told you so and you said
yeah but think of how many kids have
pissed in there.

You were yawning and it was years
since the sun went down
like it always is when the afternoons stretch out too
long and lazy
curled up at your feet.

but this was one of those tall, dark
handsome times
that they warn you about.

and I didn't want to sleep because
I didn't want to wake.

Come and get me and I would laugh
wish I was the cool water dragging at my feet
the way the night air can be empty and
full both at once
anywhere but in this skin
laugh
when you said no
what kind of sane person wades into architectural
fountains at 3 a.m.
laugh
for the life of me

come and get me
come and get me
baby,
please.

Some days
my prayers dress up as poetry
as if they are not the very same thing.

IT IS A BEAUTIFUL THING TO NEED

I come home and I am crying again. I call and tell
myself I do not need you.

how
it is a beautiful thing to need you.

I cry and google the word   relapse

I write a poem.
I leave the word   relapse

out on its own in the cold and feel bad for it.

I let it back in
kiss it like a strange and elderly uncle somewhere on my
mother's side.

I make up a stretcher for it on the floor. next to the swirls
of my hair that collect like dust

or those mandalas of hair women make on shower walls.

I cry for forty minutes because the firemen in the movie
are dead. I cry   and my boyfriend tells me I am
an ugly crier. He is not wrong but still

I go shopping for a dress for my twenty-first. I tell the
lady in the shop it must be red. I cry over the word
relapse   and eat a bowl of Honey Puffs for lunch
afterward.

On Tuesday a blog pats my shoulder. tells me to enjoy my
own company. I hand it an obscenity and eat Honey Puffs
again.

I feel small and nap for three hours.

Wednesday gets me out of bed with a thud. I evict a piece
of Monday toast and two Milkybar wrappers from my
floor. I sweep out some of the hair. take down the
stretcher.

On Thursday I remember that showers exist.

I wear things other than my duvet. realize I have had dry
eyes for three days now.   think of starting a star chart.

Friday comes home and I am not crying but it would be
ok if I were. I call because   I need you.

I make pancakes. practice yoga. remember I hate yoga. do
the washing. try piano. try being gentle.   sing a little. write a
poem.

forgive myself for being dog-eared and
lovely and   fragile   and so wonderfully and
invariably

human.

SHORT STORIES

Short stories are funny things. If I had to tell you, I would say they are the delicious moments of a half-awake morning that you will never quite remember by lunchtime. Hot coffee in cold hands. The blushed dance of avoiding collision with a stranger in the street. They are, in my humble opinion, just novels made poetry. Just life, tucked into a copper locket next to a piece of blond hair and an old newspaper clipping. Short stories are sweet, naive little creatures. They are clumsy, biased, spilling over. Erratically fiction. Invariably truth. They are all the reasons a human is capable of staying in love, and then leaves anyway.

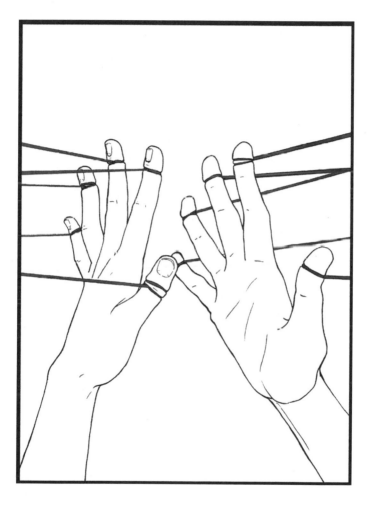

SOMEWHERE BETWEEN

I think I broke again last night
somewhere between the curl of your mouth
like smoke and now.
when I wouldn't tell you where it hurt
and the fire was purring away in the corner
throwing off all sorts of soft light
the teasing kind with the gentle edges.
and your hands I swear
were trying to find me buried in here
somewhere
I think they call it kindness
(I think they call it love)
and you were writhing and
whispered
I'm just trying to connect with you.
and
sweet thing I am so sorry.
because
me too me too
oh baby, me too.

God help me
if I would ever give up
even just one moment
of this war.

THE SEX APPEAL OF TALL BUILDINGS

Do not think of the sex appeal of tall buildings and
how long it would take. think
of the price of milk and bread and what a sweet world
where these are your worries.
think about setting your alarm how soft the morning is
brushing up against you like that how kind
the light bustling about across the floorboards humming
to herself.
make this your new favorite tune. a hymn. a prayer.
a touching of the hem.

You are an ocean that will perhaps
never stop crashing,
and
what a beautiful thing that is.

XI

Burn the house down in search of yourself.
don't you dare ever stop looking.
don't you dare
ever think you won't be worth the finding.

MARCH

It is March and the boy is sweet but altogether too soppy and nervous.

He tries to hold my hand. I laugh and spin out. car wreck. spin out and throw my hands up. grow roots into the beach. right to the magma. careering. and definitely not just trying to claim my fingers back.

this part of me. *me*. that is not his.

Later he makes an effort to sound as if he is not speaking slowly. he is pushing me on the swing. I yawn and it is deafening.

He pushes from the small of my back and asks if I enjoy my study. from the cliffs of my waist if I could ever date a doctor. from my doorframe hips and wouldn't it be strange though? too familiar? and does not let go of the hips.

I wonder if he thinks I have not noticed I am no longer moving. that his hands are pickaxes. that I am topography. mountains and gullies and rivers and ice ice ice.

I yawn again, like a bite this time. Say will you take me home now?

Are you tired?

I do not say your hands make me afraid. or I have only just noticed just how much night there is here. how very small the parking lot makes me.

The voice in my head says *drama queen*. rolls her eyes.

sits still as a cat. He hovers on my breasts like a question and I nearly burst out laughing. vomit. I am not overly familiar with first-date etiquette but I do not think this is it.

Yes, I am tired. early start tomorrow and all.

We are both ignoring his hands as if my skin were a dead thing. not a *mine* at all.

Ok.

He sounds hurt and I struggle not to feel guilty.

We are quiet on the drive back. I try not to hear it as
an apology for my body.

try not to think about being glad that he starts the car.
drives in the right direction.

You write like a wailing thing.
like a thing caught on fire.

MY HOME IS ACHING

I wept a continent onto your chest last night
let you stroke my hair
hand me soft mutterings

if you bite your lip and do not breathe
you can almost sound as if you are not tearing apart
completely

and it is good to be held when your edges
are all fraying
unraveled
and it is good to have a boy who says
"baby, look at me
see how beautiful you are
I love you so very much"
tells you to unwrap your arms
do not cradle yourself away from me like that
says   please
and means my home is aching.

and I am sorry that I was crying
heaving
softly
excruciatingly softly

even you, sweet human
do not want to see me guttural and
retching

there is an empty space at the bottom of my road
between the lights
and some nights I let it hold me
bite my fists
scream and scream into the upholstery
marvel at the canyons that form down my neck

and it is good to be held when your edges are long gone
have a boy who thinks he is gentling the shore and not
the ocean

this book is an honest thing
so I will rest in the crook of its neck
and tell you that I think of the height of cranes
and how long they would take to climb
of ropes and water
of sharp edges and the meaning of the word mercy

I will tell you
(as I tell myself; draped in kindness)
of how I have spent a lifetime of tall dark nights
breaking into pieces
and still risen again in the morning.

II

You are a wild,

                unkempt thing.

the poetry will come later.

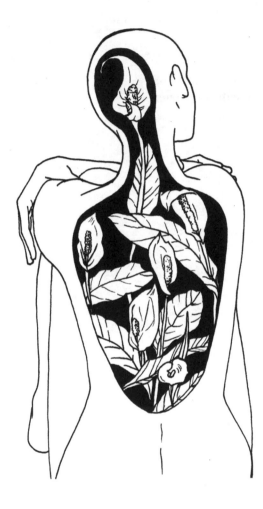

Sometimes it is a very sad thing
to be human
and longing
oh,
but if we weren't.

A HAT TRICK

Where you are the hat and the rabbit and the white gloves
and all of the magic. I will pull out this voice for you until
you are reconciled with your own throat.

I am a medical student and so I tell you honestly,
we are made only of stories
of borrowed limbs
people we have loved.

every stranger's smile and
checking of the mailbox on the way home.

you
human
which is to say piece of art

which is to say
thank God
for this thing that hurts is the only difference between
living and being

alive.

XII

You thank me for the poems.
though it is you with these words
in your mouth.

NEIL THINKS THAT ART AND MENTAL ILLNESS ARE THE VERY SAME THING

Neil Hilborn writes about his fourth love and wanting to
die. I have a mother on her third.
she was engaged once but she threw away the ring. had to
give back all the gifts. her father did
but she has not, so far as I'm aware,
wanted to die. at least
not so strongly as to tell her child about it. which is to say
that maybe she has.

I am on my first. it is something like sharing limbs and I
think that I will never stop bleeding if he leaves. or if I do.
but then so did Neil, probably.
perhaps we grow back like starfish. make ourselves a new
body. forget to catch ourselves before we are suddenly
walking around with someone else's hand or leg.

I just sat outside on the grass for twenty-three minutes.
read poetry about dying and not. called it mindfulness.

Neil thinks that art and mental illness are the very same
thing.

Me and my stepsister used to tell checkout ladies at the
supermarket that we were twins, and I think it is
something like that.
or when I used to take the clay from the stream behind
the house and make it into bowls that my mother
refused to keep. fish for eels with a shoelace.
touch someone's shoulder before speaking.
apologize with my eyes.
forever love with whatever parts of me were and are
and will be
left.

46 THREADS

I carry threads in me
covered in handwriting / probably the terrible sort
if it is mine
or maybe it is God's
letters would be the size of buildings / the shape of
honesty, if there is such a thing.

The handwriting is beside the point.
I carry threads in me
and written on these are the reasons my fingernails
grow faster than my mother's
how I have her teeth / but my father's sigh.

Written on these are the reasons why
I cry out oceans that only fill up my eyes some more
and
write like breathing

And I am starting to wonder
if these last two are perhaps the very same thing.

I try my best not to be afraid
of the days
when I am all light.

SUMMER TWO YEARS AGO

Izzie is singing
a voice that is rattling each of us while we pretend not
to be listening
and Boaz
is on the drum set in the corner
and I'm sad a little but not

not the way summer two years ago took up all the
room in my body
squeezed me out
they're rehearsing for a wedding
like how last night I dreamed it was mine and took
hours on the vows kept crying but not
the summer two years ago kind.

It's a fuzzy thing
one that you can't keep your hands around
wake up and it's your own
gentle neck
it's your own head
but not the *maybe I'll have toast* sort of thought
you will become a black hole
falling and fallen
all gulped up but also the hole

and the climb out takes years but then one day
in early March
your wedding singer friends will rehearse
and you will look out at a lake that swallows up the
sunset the same way you do
and you will have two years of poetry
a borrowed deck chair that is growing to remember
the shape of you
some sort of ladder
out of that hole
that was not you, not
even slightly,
after all.

Good poetry,
truly good poetry,
is nearly always a person.

SEPTEMBER

September mornings
and the way your mother used to hum
tried to teach you to make bread
knead it or it won't ripen
it was good with soup
and good
for hands in winter
even though she'd never made one
that didn't break apart

My father lost his words
on my second birthday
when I was only just finding mine
and I used to go out to lie in the old hammock
close my eyes
trail bare feet through the wandering dew
listen to it whispering back

these are poems

you can feel them soft
in your hands

you can pull them out of yourself

find that you are made of
Russian nesting dolls
fabric that will not ever stop coming
out from your sleeve

they can teach you a lot
if you use the words gently
like how staying can look like many things
and loving can look like more

how it is important
to teach your daughter to make the bread
carry her voice in her hands
shrug off her boots after the rain in that special way that lets
her keep her socks on
apologize
with your eyes if your mouth stops working
and always
always
to forgive

(have I ever told you that;
how you carry that word so entirely)

FOR ALL OF MY LIFETIMES

She would whisper of how the sun woke
how she could feel it
humming right through the curtains
and she would tell me to run to it.
and we would.
every time we would.
and I used to love the way her laugh
always got so caught up in her hair.
how she was never good
at staying out of the ocean
like I was.
how she would have carried me
for all of my lifetimes
bundled up
into her palms
if she could have.

Privilege.
to have lived inside such a soft storm
as my mother.

IF ONLY YOU LET YOUR RIBS SING

I find it in the quiet
strum along
if only you let your ribs sing.
let yourself
break into rivers.
drown the cracks in the hungry earth.
the ones wider than your own.

the trees are always kindest when spring comes.
so let the soil into your nose
teach yourself the hymns again
teach yourself to sow
know that the words help. and the unwashed hands.

it's all just love and birdsong in your lungs anyway.
but this earth, oh
this earth will be the one that
brings me back.

What soft violence;
to choose to be happy.
to choose to be kind.

IN FIFTY YEARS

I swear every tender morning it's as if
your eyes have been holding the world together overnight.
a string of balloons.
that's the me part of this
I think
the string.

say the word and we can carry this house away.
home, rather.
how jazz makes you frightfully angry
and in love
and your eyes blaze in that way that
they do.

do you remember sending me that photo of your cereal
last April?
the one by the lawn
autumn laid out like clean sheets and longing.
how you said she looked just like me?

I just know
we'll be sitting outside on the veranda
the one that won't stop darn squeaking

moss clinging to us and these
sweet old chairs.
you'll probably be humming the blues
still

and the sun will be older and softer
in that bathtub sky
but baby,
not us.
I hope we beat the door down
still
dance until our bodies give out
I hope we forever love
with our mouths open and our hearts
full full full.

I think I could love you well in German.
in the rain.
against ripped backseat car upholstery.

MY MOTHER ASKS IF YOU KNOW GOD

My mother asks if you know God.
I tell her / no / but
on our third date I told you we wouldn't have sex
and you stayed. so, I guess that's close?

> I am naked to the waist and there is a forest fire starting
> beneath my ear.

Jasper laughs and drinks beer as it spills over us says
"Jamie, have you gon' converted my boy?"

because he breathes the forest. and tramping. the quiet noise.
we go swimming in waterfalls and all I do is tell him that
my word for this is God.

the falling in love he does on his own.

at six months he looks at me, calls me love. realizes that
this, too, is faith.

> I am molten against the length of him

my dad stopped going when his ex-wife got custody of the
church.

who knew you could feel everything in just
two hands

he listens to the music and cries

and that boy's mouth

he tells me that he cannot see forever
without me in it

and that boy's heart

he is every amen I have ever laid down on lips

this is not a proposal

but if this life is an altar. the sacrifice is little. and the
love

is so
so great.

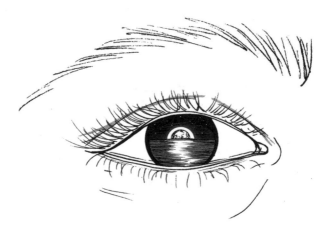

You are
the ocean open mouth kissing
the moon.
the rain on an upturned face
on the parched Atacama earth.
you are the pitch of the night sky
before your eyes adjust
but then;
just see how much light it holds.

YOUR BARE FEET

The kitchen is a dance (not metaphor, I swear). The kitchen
is a dance and your bare feet.
You are Louis Armstrong. "La Vie En Rose."
I am sick which calls for soup because of our grandmothers.

I have seven seconds of watching your happy before you
see me looking. which is to say your happiness is free.

two strides and *there is no such thing as too sick for dancing*
and your hands are mountains up the back of me
I am all cliff-face and
now waltz and saxophone and God I love you so much
when you wear it on your face like that.

My nose is against your neck and you smell of home.
dancing while the soup boils over. bare feet and a blocked
nose and your hair caught in my fingers and God, I love you
so.

ODE TO THE POETRY BOOK

You
the inside of someone else.
soft lace collar and
all gentle
I am sorry I do not have more time
for your
smell of autumn and
op-shop
pages
your long-loved mosaic
museum past
the story of someone else with the same
skin and hands
as me
forever staring out windows romanticizing
carrying around their great dream-heads
holding
falling in love with
the careful weight of you
all of you
in their lap.

PAUL THOMAS

I think we have the same eyes.
the way Sundays sit heavy at our heels
in the pits of our stomachs
(like the way our mothers would tell us
we'd grow gardens out our ears
from swallowing the seeds
and we
never much minded).
the point is it was 9 p.m. for you
and Saturday for me
and really what better thing did I have to do
than pour myself out
across the continents through a phone line.

You always sounded like gravel
and you told me
I'm a Pisces. it means I've lived many lives. I think that's
why.
and I said
well maybe you still are.
anyway,
I hope you do go looking for it.
that's the important part. when I moaned

about our day jobs and moving out to the country. and you
swore
you'd build us a tree house and live
far far above it all.
and then there's the children.

Because I'm an addict. (why you didn't
just do it)
and maybe me too.
you've got to see how beautiful it is
or that's when it'll get ya
fucked, for sure.
but beautiful or what the hell are we all doing here
anyway.
the way the cramped city glow
sticks to the back of your eyelids.
shuts the stars out
but
always takes you home
holds the door of your cab open.
and then there's the drinking.

She was a genius, absolutely.
but she broke your heart
tried to do it gently (and who the
fuck wants that)
so you broke it back. only kissed

the girl, but still.

You'd already done your mourning
by the time you told me.
shrugged as you handed it over but
pressed it down
hard into my hands so I would know.
you've always got to see the damn thing
and I love that about you.
how beautiful it must have been
(fuck, we were so in love, you know?)
to make up for the rest of this
hellhole.

It's easier said than done
this unlearning
this
unfurling
of the bones.

There is a mountain in me
it is weather-beaten and on Sundays
a heap of coal
fearful
but still,
wonderfully made
and by the morning day in and out
like lace curtains
fingers in hair and on elbow bends

by the morning I am a summit.

by the morning I am a triumph.

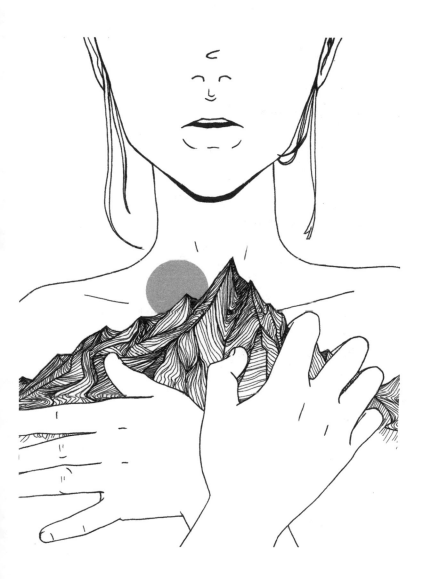

AUTUMN

The nights have started to curl
back into themselves
autumn creeping slowly under
my fingernails
hands like a hearth in yours
in an old Vonnegut novel
that's seen better days
and worse.

It's always been like this;
home will turn vermilion and warm
crisp at the edges
start to look more and more
like you.

There are words playing hooky in the back of your throat. the kind this book is full of.
the kind that belong in your mouth.

HOME IS THOSE SATURDAY COBBLES

I brought Blue
told him New York
like I meant my place or yours?
and maybe I had

and then there's Paul Thomas
the capitalized Writer
who we'll meet by the Hudson.
We'll probably skip stones
talk music and Smith Coronas
and he'll have that nebula wink in his eye
that laugh like a brother
(and perhaps neither of us will ever
know where we first met)

I'll probably walk in circles under
autumn palms
cry at how beautiful the brickwork is
try to find Sylvia Plath in
old bookstores
search for home in the soft
of woodsmoke
I'll probably find that it is beautiful
all ridiculously beautiful

and I'll brush the poems up
off the sidewalk
meet them in bars that feel like an exhale
sashay through them
in Times Square

gentle them
into soft brown parcels
and try to send them back

and I'll pretend I had almost forgotten
the address of
home
the cobbles that are always too cold
on Saturday morning feet
and the way your hair makes its way
into my fingers each evening
the warmth of your mouth
on my forehead

I'll pretend I had almost forgotten
when I've long since known
that home
is always only and utterly
you.

THE PORTRAIT SELLER ON FIFTH

If you sit with her, she will write you.
find where your edges fold
by hers.
press you into the margins print you outward
by the dog with the itch
the children in toe-to-toe tourist formation
the man that sleeps under his own music.
and you won't always see it
like she will.
and you can ask but she will seldom tell you
of the pieces she has taken.

of the pieces she has given back.

YOUNG SPRING

I chew a hole in the side of my thumb thinking about
your mouth
wedding dresses
an entire night of high heels minus the bleeding feet.

I sit on the deck in the early sun in the
sweet breeze lake air young spring young skin
and am homesick for this moment

think about the things we get to keep
I hope it is hands
eighty years of wrinkled smile love
grandchildren

my mother wants six
I look at the job that walks me home at 6 p.m. and
know I have already left it
the mothers on the playground
the headiness of a summer and not having any place to
be

you look at me and it is something like soft fire
taking the rubbish out
buying milk and the paper on Saturdays

staying up late to welcome the year in

I sit on the deck in the early sun in the
sweet breeze lake air young spring young skin
and the children are down for their nap and
the whole house smells like new bread and rain and
your hand is on my ankle and
your mouth tastes like summer the sun hands us freckles
rosy cheekbones and sunblocked noses and
this is home
a thousand times over,
this is home.

Today is by far the most beautiful creature
I have ever come across.

MORE LIKE RAIN

Love me
more rain than summer days
more
shivering to our bones but laughing into each other's hair
all the same

more like hiding under that old maple
on Sixth breathing up against the heat of each other
throwing bread crumbs
hazy voices
out into the Avon
skipping stones and flowers and
backstories

pretending to be capable of thinking of anything other than
the way your mouth curls upward like smoke
upward
like an invitation.

There are many things that will fit
beneath your skin
if yours is the type to house winter.
if you are more parts storm than
organs.
if you are spring cleaning
the empty attic.
I promise
forgiveness does not take up much room.

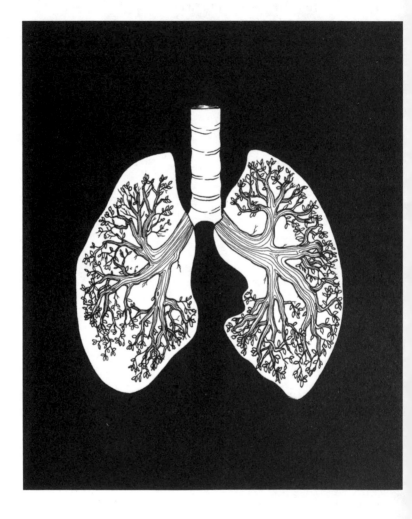

Some days you will breathe
and
it will be enough.

COLD HARD HANDS AND ALL THE ONES THAT DIDN'T STAY

There are days when you shiver.
can I tell you now that you don't have to have
tall dark stories.
of cold hard hands and all the ones
that didn't stay. but they
can help. they can
brood in your bones. those things
that you hardly remember.

or they can belong to someone else.
leave you
throwing heaving sobs out with nowhere
to put them. you always liked
the word *abyss*.
tiptoe so that you do not break.
that vertigo of looking
down. or was it
back?

What I am saying
is that there are many ways of telling
a story.
and not all of them are kind.

and not all of them are true.
even when you whisper them softly
against yourself. echolocation.
listen
to see what is still in there.
ok,
but some of them
aren't so bad. there are special ways of telling it.
like *it was a long time ago*. and how
always
some people have it worse.
the point is it can be nothing
just grumbly neurons
just the weather
little white pills next to your cereal bowl.

One way to tell a story:
my mother is afraid of her brother
and so I've never met him. she sends him
birthday messages on Facebook. wonders
if he still lives in that
Tough Old Place.

my father's grandfather.
my mother's father.
we don't talk about those ones
but maybe we should.

At twelve I deleted my search history
because depression
was a dirty word and I had a perfectly
perfectly good life.
and people will read this who know me
and don't
and will tell me oh, but
that was such *a long time ago*.

and if it shouldn't have affected you because
you had wanted it
they hadn't meant it like that
you're just too sensitive
too soft
that happens to everybody
it was an accident
but they apologized

because
both of your parents were so good
so good about the leaving
the being left

that doesn't mean it didn't.

A SMALL MERCY

You may well find yourself still
held
to the gentle of my wrists
still
mouth-pressed
up against that skin
like
stained glass windows.
like forgiveness.

You do not have to hold it
quite so very tightly;
this light that is already yours.

There is a prayer in me,
still.

FOR THE LIFE OF US

You scare me a little. the way you're never quite close
enough
and the days are that stern old lady
a high school dance / beating us apart with a wooden
ruler.
slashing through the itchy kind of grass out in the woods.
that
is how this feels. fingertips only.

I think I loved you when the rain came.
when you told me
"I've learned this, and those are cumulus
and they are just the sweet kind" and then right as we
were walking back the skies dropped it on us.
wholeheartedly.
and we were both wearing my sweaters
both laughing like we couldn't stop.
and for the life of us I swear we couldn't.

your arms were around me
and the threadbare tree that you claimed was shelter was
around you.
and you gave me your laughing mouth

like you had loved me
all your life.

sometimes you whisper my name
and I think that it's the same
for you.
the way our skin holds us apart.
how I want to shatter
inside of you.

if you speak in silences
then broken
means just the same as welcome.
just the same as
oh please won't you stay.

XIII

I write out the parts of me that make me soft
to keep them in pockets
toss into fountains
make wishes on.
to remember how it hurt
but see
how lovely they have made me.
see how kind.

A great many things can become poems
if you just hold them hard enough.

HOMESICK

Just like that—
how a body can be yours
and loved
and then something else entirely

shape-shifter
wandering
I am homesick again
though I do not like to call it lost.

do you remember
somewhere in the origami between your ears
of when I asked why you loved me
why this
precise collection of
organs

I was being cute
and I probably should have told you that
before
prepared your mouth
but I just asked
hoped you would know from my eyes
or the way I was holding my bones
cradling
that I needed a pretty little nothing from you.

you called me broken.
sweet honest
heartbreaking boy.
you called me your wee broken thing.
I think I laughed
made some kind of noise at least
definitely not like a wounded animal
hinges at night
but my veins were all jam
sludged up
whacking into the walls of me
and my face was fine just fine just
if you think the words like this all together and quick
your head will not have time
to pause
break
water the gardens in your eyes

the thing is
that
broken things
us mosaics
do not like to be told so
and especially not loved so

and now all I can think about are the
things
that make up my insides
paint out the word l o v e on the ceiling like

a triumph
make me sexy the way only words and rain can be
at least big enough wide enough
whole
enough
to hold another heart

and whether or not I am simply more parts fiction
more parts poetry
than me.

Some mornings,
the kind sort,
hold more autumn
than human. more gentling.
more soft in the bones.

And so
this book
shall become my confessional.

September is streaming in
bursting upward
making rivers of me
and I imagine that I am embroidery
the lace of the curtains
swaying with the inhale.
this air
that has not seen rain for weeks.

ANOTHER POEM FOR A CULTURE I AM NOT

I am trying to think of what would fill out this body if not bones and flesh. if not blood. the people and the places in me.

There are languages that leave my mouth empty. I try to find the word for home and it is not there. I like to think there is no *reo* word for empty but mouths are very good at filling up the spaces. the rifts. even when there are none.

Still. I can roll it around beneath my tongue like river stones. count. try not to catch a waiata between my teeth on the way out.

There are signposts in my country with words that start with *Ngā*. The sounds trace the land like cracked hands. *Taonga*. I claim back small pieces of myself as we drive through. *Ngāruawāhia*. There is a marae here that feels like a church. My mother teaches me how to whisper under my breath as if *te reo* is an accident.

Korero. Māori used to name birds for their voices, for their songs. *Te Koeti*. I curl my tongue around the sounds of places not in me. *Matua*. I am still finding my throat.

SOME SORT OF VOW

I promise to forever give you more poetry
than I take.

THE MEMORIES I BELONG TO

Sometimes I wonder where I am held
what memories I belong to
soft at the wrist the mouth
on strange continents like hands we used to call home
cerebral attics and pressed petal pages
under the familiar creak of an old mattress
old bedhead

I hope I am the new sheets
the smell of fresh timber
the way your laugh catches you off guard flits around
the room like it does not quite belong to you
the freckle above your elbow
the young men following strangers' wars along the top
shelf of the bookstore on Twelfth
the books you keep for me

I hope I am in the books
I hope I am
I hope

NOISE

I am more silent vigor savor the evening still
not my father's
wearing of business like a backbone
mother's
noise
I am
leave poetry in old footprints to find like lucky pennies
water the garden on Tuesdays
blue curtains that are just blue curtains.

Writing:
that soft magic of making something
heavier and lighter
both at once.

ON CLAIMING THINGS THAT ARE NOT OURS

I do try, Sarah
to be courageous. to know things and
write like I know things
of Hemingway and cigarettes and bar top cartwheels
and streets that can be called Twelfth.

here it is summer, though Christmas.
the earth calls me
a second-hand sunrise baited breath a christening
soil marking knees and elbows as territory
and I call it home right back.

my street is Aberdeen, which I suppose is pretty if you
were to meet it as a stranger.
everything dances in that easy sway that serenades
an evening breeze.
I fall asleep to the hum and whir of a
bedside fan.

I do try, Sarah
although there are no Vietnam and Libya here.
no smoky bar
(and I never much liked whiskey)

I write poetry sipping on milk with pajamas and wet hair.

I write poetry in what is perhaps the same way we all
make amends
apologize with our hands
tether ourselves to yesterday and tomorrow and this
goddamn beautiful being alive business
all at once.

Stretch upward, little garden.
dip your fingers into the sun like honey.

A SLOW FIRE

I would very much like
to be forever
stirring against you in the soft of the small hours
a slow fire
the hum of a refrigerator
ocean
a hallway light
singing the words wrong on purpose
the smell of pine
a staircase that makes us fall in love with the house
spring
the way the warmth of you tapers in at my waist and
ankles and neck
and
mouth.

Oh, what poetry you will be.

"A LITERARY REVENGE IS THE MOST HUMILIATING OF ALL PUNISHMENTS"

That is a quote by Hera Lindsay Bird. I did not say that.
I read it in the book *Hera Lindsay Bird.*
says the well-meaning friend poet trying to scrabble
away from copyright issues.

But I do agree. I do pump up the bellows of my insides
and deep somewhere is an old inky ashy fire. sluggish
in the basement that no one goes into including me
because perhaps it is haunted.

Hera Lindsay Bird talks about sex a lot. uses a ruder
word for it. and it fascinates me
to have one hundred eleven pages of metaphor and still
be liked. to write about a sitcom and still be the poet in
the newspaper. to write about slitting your wrists but
in a funny way.

Hera Lindsay Bird is the type of writer I do not wholly
want to be friends with, but want a share of her limbs
all the same. just a few fingers to pull out at
Thanksgiving and particularly ironic reality TV moments.

Poem one is about pissing her pants in a grocery store.
the bravery in that, huh. when the book happens to fall

open to Pandora's box of embarrassing confessions and
then oops it is only the first page.

I need more of Hera Lindsay Bird's pre-laugh. the calling
the joke early so the reader gets that the funny bits are
less funny when it is not actually a snakeskin negligee. a
kite factory. righteous indignation.

a stranger feeling along the back of your throat for a
flashlight.

My mother has been teaching me to
break out in poetry
for as long as I can remember.

THE WAY YOU ARE A HALLELUJAH

You can be
a good thing and not a whole thing
the way you are a hallelujah like that

it is Christmas Eve
a chorus of angels
my Nana buttering the toast wrong
an argument about turkey and cholesterol
and yet this is love

I covet December
when they will sing Jesus accidentally
but without shrinking

my boyfriend
is every amen I have laid down on lips
eyelashes worshipping skin
the bowing hands

and this is love
God, how this is love.

A SMALL MIRACLE

That these animal bodies are capable
of such an anchoring
this sleepy burn
this sharing of limbs.

ON HOW I DECIDE WHICH OF US IS TO BECOME THE POEM

The poem is a hurting thing,
and I hope it is not me but God,
I hope it is not you.

THE VERY SAME THING

There are some things
that fit against your bones / the space
behind your ears
better or worse than others like autumn leaves / falling
but still vermilion
which is not to say they do not
fit but
I don't think I'll ever not cry at the soft curve
the young moon of a wrist / and I don't want to claim this
as your fault but

a certain kind of proof:

you
the splintering of a heart
the end of the world
(which may or may not all be the very same thing)

There are flowers in my chest again
the kind
that do not lose their bloom.

LOVE POEMS

It is not Saturday night. cold
and hunched on a wooden floor up against the fire.
I have been reading love poems again
and thinking of the bridge between your index finger
and thumb. how the soft that can be found
collected on you
would be enough for all of our winters
if only you let me keep them.

and it is not a leaving
not if you say yes. give someone a small collection of
bones to hold in their small collection of bones.
and skin.
to put a small band of metal around.
exchange
for the tender in your mornings.
all the mornings for the rest of your life.

It is not Saturday night in an unreasonably freezing
house in Hamilton where you are not.
and I am not being dramatic
which is to say that it is just a fireplace and not
the rocking hips of a wedding dance.
just a fire.

I kiss you through a sliver of doorway so that the cat
doesn't get out. it seems

a terribly mundane thing to be doing
practically folding the washing
plucking the single black hair off your shoulder
blade.

and yet
like everything else
it is love.
It is a Saturday night and I am in love
and I hope you will let me give this to you.

The rain comes and sounds like you. I let it slip out
of my hand
a scarf billow
an open doorway
the blur of a coat and a wave and a leaving
that does not become a goodbye
until the after.

WHEN THEY ASK ABOUT VENICE BEACH

Venice Beach is the girl who will look at you like
laughter as she begs a crystal to her lips.
the man
in three duvets and half a backpack who worships a
Los Angelean sky.
two pugs in a stroller.

the lady with the vivacious orange hair and the listless
orange coat.
"shitty advice" for a dollar.
the confused dress code of facial hair and denim and
pants down to your knees.
the boy yelling "ooh girl how you *doin*'" just like off
every American movie I've ever seen.

underwear with customizable obscenities across the front.
Chris on his typewriter. weed.
and the piano man.
the healers. the twin blond boys with the big green
sunnies and too-long bangs.
an introvert's sweating palms.

It is the balloon animals and the dogs and the
bodybuilders holding hands
and the legs and the painters and the dreadlocks and the
skaters and the band that plays for lunch. it is the struggle
it is the struggle it is the struggle

but good God, it is the triumph.

THIS LAND IS MY CHURCH
first published in *Indigo*

See over there between the trees
where the light blinks stained glass windows
and

the sun
waves good morning, how are you this fine Sunday
would you like a newsletter
and

the grass bows into that soft carpet
the type that's hard to move chairs on
and

the soft white of the clouds will tumble
over you
the pastor's words the smile of his wife
and

you will inhale the air and close your eyes
feel the stillness against your palms
and

of course,
then there is always the food the tea

the breaking of bread

you can be sad lonely as defeated as you like
but there will always be
the bread.

DAY 1278

I cannot tell you why I still trust God
to a fault
except that the pills do not always work and
neither do the prayers but
at least they are always listened to.

at least they are always wept with.

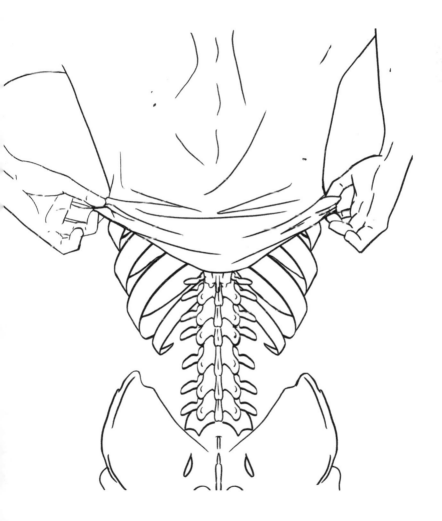

157

A PART POEM

and I find them;
the tiptoeing bones we call love and
let inside of ourselves.
shuffling down our limbs and into our open mouths.
and suddenly all of the rest of it is irrelevant.
and all that is left and good and whole is that your skin
is home, and that with you
I am so desperately understood.

FRIENDLY REMINDER

A relapse is not a coming home.

DEPRESSION IS A PARK BENCH

Depression is a park bench.
the slope of aging wood. moss. the cracks.
the old man who has lost his wife but will keep his
dog longer than his lungs.

depression is rain on a roof. the kind you cannot
hear. but everything is wet come morning.

depression is the Christmas tree dying in the corner.
until March. we threw last year's into another tree
that has now grown around it. cornflakes for breakfast
every day for a year. learning not to hate the pills—it
was probably just their upbringing.

I will not say that depression is hope. but you have
worshipped the cold tile of a bathroom floor with your
forehead many times, and that is at least something.

depression is this poem. which is to say anxious. which
is to say pleading. which is to say God, it is a slow
process but you will come out of this so good and so
whole and so

so very brave.

THE BEST ADVICE I KNOW

Find peace
and build a home out of it.

THE NIGHT WE WOULD HAVE BEEN
BADASS IF WE WEREN'T JUST SINGING
ABBA IN A PARKING LOT

Driving with your head out the window is really good for
depression.
Ideally fast, and in Molly's just-a-friend Harrison's new
Audi.
There is a five-thousand-dollar stereo that will give you a
new pulse and
is a lot better than silence.
The Audi is a good investment despite the current
housing crisis and a
forty-thousand-dollar student loan.
You cannot caress the city out a window by paying off a
student loan.

Drive to the museum with the lawn and the stage light
haze. It looks like the word *grand*. Like a good choice if
you were to become a building.
You will lose your shoes
run like you haven't in months and
near break your body to reach your torso out the
sunroof.
Pretend you are a coming-of-age
New York movie
where she gets the guy and paints herself the color of
ambition.

She also does not shrug on mental illness with her shoes in
the morning.

Whoop into the night
offer your arms up
catch the wind in your hair your ears
the corners of your eyes
pretend you are not only driving through the museum
parking lot with your head loud with something other than
you for once
your hands holding enough night air to craft a new set of
lungs
because
like hell that's all this is.

It's all poetry,
if you believe in that sort of thing.

165

I AM

I read about a gay Chinese boy who writes poetry about
being gay and Chinese.
a West African prostitute who loses her mother but
learns a savior's tongue.
grandfather of Vietnam and Libya.

I read about a gay Chinese boy
and wonder what letters I can drag out of old bones.
the genealogy of this
precise
collection of organs

I would let you in if only you asked
throw open big pearl gates
rows of teeth
read out of a throat that breaks despite a good childhood
upbringing

I am less *white* more
I wear the freckles of my mother along my wrists and
elbows
the ridges behind my ears.

less *woman* but
never   less.

I am my father's quiet brave and
the smell of my grandmother's house in the morning
which is to say the sky before seven
bread and soft hands.

I am well-off household
thank God, money for Ruth
the therapy
the easy stumble
all of the blessing and still the
fall
risc
triumph.

I am heterosexual cis would-sometimes-prefer-a-darker-
more-vogue-shade-of-white
blessed assortment of heartbreak
woman
and this

this

is my poetry.

I dare you not to call it flirting
the way a bookstore will hug against the back of you
breathe behind your ears.

THE MORAL OF POETRY

The moral of poetry is waking on Christmas. old jazz in a
new living room. slow dancing with your eyes foggy and
damp as a storm.

the most delicious concession;
this sharing of a body. goosebumped and naked.
using the word *fuck* and meaning
baby, I have never held anything that felt so much like
home as you.

poetry is walking too soon when the traffic lights take
too long. closing your eyes at the back of the church.

the first flicker of morning eyes when your throat is
caught by the boy on the pillow next to you. he will say
vulnerable like it is not a cuss and you
will feel the word *love* unfurl from under your tongue.

poetry is your not-yet boyfriend dropping kebab
into the hole in the crotch of his pants.
telling the lady at the perfume counter that you want the
smell of autumn and slept-in sheets,   please.

it is Plath and Frost and
Bukowski *living so well that death trembles to take him*
it is my six-year-old brother

(Homage to Charles Bukowski)

171

A Long time ago There lived Lonly Sunflower that wantend a freind. Her name was poem... Her name

it is my inability to ever end a poem, or rather
anything at all, in a satisfactory way

the old-style movie reel
pooling on the ground between us in a cozy velvet
theater the color of fidelity in the first house we ever
bought and never left and

     there is never an end.

thank God,

     there is never an end.

ABOUT THE AUTHOR

F. D. Soul is a New Zealand author and poet with an intrepid love of the air before 7 a.m. and climbing through brass window frames.

You can find her on Instagram @featherdownsoul, in the garden, or at her mother's house.

P.S. Thank you.